CHRIS VAN WYK
MY MOTHER'S LAUGHTER

My Mother's Laughter
SELECTED POEMS

Chris van Wyk

Edited by
Ivan Vladislavić & Robert Berold

deep
south

ISBN 978-1-928476-32-0
ebook ISBN 978-1-928476-33-7

Deep South
contact@deepsouth.co.za
www.deepsouth.co.za

Distributed in South Africa by
University of KwaZulu-Natal Press
www.ukznpress.co.za

Distributed worldwide by
African Books Collective
PO Box 721, Oxford, OX1 9EN, UK
www.africanbookscollective.com/publishers/deep-south

Cover design: Benjamin Stanwix
Text design and layout: Liz Gowans
Cover photo: TJ Lemon/*The Star* 1 June 1996

Contents

from the Uncollected Poems

Introduction

For much of the 1980s, Chris van Wyk was the editor of *Staffrider*. This literary and cultural magazine was established at Ravan Press in 1978 in response to the new writing that emerged after the Soweto student uprising – 'the great surge of creative activity which has been one of the more hopeful signs of recent times', as the first editorial put it. While the focus was on new voices, rooted in community cultural groups, the magazine also attracted a wide range of 'unattached' contributors, producing poetry, fiction, popular history, graphics and photographs. The young Van Wyk, who had already published a collection of poetry and started his own literary magazine *Wietie*, took over the reins of *Staffrider* in 1980 and brought his own ideas to it.

When I joined the press a few years later, Chris was the first person I got to know. On my first morning in the job, he offered to show me around and soon set me at ease. Ravan operated out of an old house in O'Reilly Road in Berea and an outbuilding served as storage for the overflow of books. Chris took me up a wooden ladder into the attic of this storeroom, which was piled with books and magazines. As he began to speak about his work, it became clear that for him *Staffrider* was the heart of the enterprise.

Many readers would have agreed. Although the press had a diverse publishing list, ranging from children's books to academic history, *Staffrider* had a unique magnetic appeal. Young writers from all over the Reef arrived at the door, clutching poems or stories handwritten in exercise books or on scraps of paper. Chris spent part of nearly every day at the kitchen table or on a bench in the back yard, going over edited pages with these visitors. Editing had been kept to a minimum in the early days of the magazine, but by now Chris was intent on improving the quality of the work he published, and poured his energies into the task. He became a mentor and friend to countless emerging writers and artists.

*

Chris van Wyk was born in Johannesburg in 1957, the eldest of six children. After a few years in Newclare, his family moved to Riverlea, a small coloured township between the city and Soweto, loomed over by a mine dump. He would spend much of his life in Riverlea, which he later described as a 'forgotten township'.

His first poems were published in the *Star* newspaper in 1975 when he was still a matric student at Riverlea High School, and he continued writing and publishing through the intense political and cultural ferment of the Soweto uprising of June 1976. Recalling this time decades later, he asserted: 'I am of the 1976 generation of poets.'

His early work was shaped by the Black Consciousness movement and was defiant in its call for resistance and change. Alongside these forceful political poems, he also produced tender, sensual love poems, many dedicated to his high-school sweetheart Kathy (they married in 1980 and had two sons, Kevin and Karl).

He showed his first writings to poets Stephen Gray and Robert Greig, who gave him advice and encouragement. His debut collection, *It Is Time to Go Home*, published by Ad Donker in 1979 when Chris was 22, announced him as a writer of unusual promise, and won the Olive Schreiner Prize.

Despite this early recognition, Chris's focus moved away from poetry. In 1982, he published *A Message in the Wind*, a children's book that won a Maskew Miller Longman award. Many other books for children followed over the years, including widely read tales like *Petroleum and the Orphaned Ostrich* and *Ouma Ruby's Secret*.

In the late 1970s, he worked for the South African Committee for Higher Education (Sached) writing material for newly literate adults, a job he left in 1980 to found the literary magazine *Wietie* with his friend Fhazel Johennesse. Later that year, he went to work for Ravan Press.

He was passionate about promoting literacy and reading, and never turned down an invitation to speak to schoolchildren, who were enthralled by his stories and his infectious way of telling them. After the advent of democracy, a publisher commissioned him to write a series of short readable biographies of prominent figures in the South African political struggle. These were prescribed in schools and led to unexpected financial success, allowing him to give up his work as a freelance editor and write full-time.

The following years saw the publication of his memoir *Shirley, Goodness & Mercy* (2004) and its sequel *Eggs to Lay, Chickens to Hatch* (2010), which put Riverlea on the map and brought him a wide readership. While he enjoyed the acclaim, what mattered most was the local response, the reactions of old schoolfriends, neighbours, shopkeepers. He loved telling how people contacted him to correct a detail or challenge a conclusion, or – best of all – to complain that they weren't in the book.

Chris's other publications included the novel *The Year of the Tapeworm* (1996), an English translation of A.H.M.

Scholtz's *Vatmaar* (2000), and a biography of the activist Bill Jardine, *Now Listen Here* (2003). He was also commissioned to abridge Mandela's *Long Walk to Freedom* for young readers. He was working on a novel when he died of cancer in 2014.

*

Although he continued to write poetry into the 1990s, Van Wyk did not publish another collection after *It Is Time to Go Home*. He incorporated ten poems into his memoirs – five of them from the *It Is Time* volume – using them to tell parts of his story and describing the contexts in which they were written. This selection aims to present the best of this published and unpublished work to new readers, and to older readers who are only familiar with the long-out-of-print first collection.

The qualities that make his prose so engaging are also evident in his poetry. He was drawn to aphorisms and puns and adroitly extended metaphors or plays on words. He also had a gift for capturing a child's view of the world, and some poems are imbued with a childlike sense of wonder that transcends the cute and sentimental.

He was a wonderful storyteller, acutely observant and attuned to how South Africans speak. He was alive to the world of working people – some of his most memorable stories and poems play out in taxis and train compartments – and he knew how to capture the spontaneity and earthiness of a spoken story on the page.

All this makes for memorable writing: lines and images stick in the mind years after they have been heard or read. Several poems, including 'A Riot Policeman', 'About Graffiti', 'We Can't Meet Here, Brother' and 'The Ballot and the Bullet' have been widely anthologized. 'In Detention' has found its place in the South African canon and the popular memory: with its chilling permutations, it remains one of the starkest indictments of apartheid's duplicity and brutality in our literature.

*

Thanks are due to Karl van Wyk and Kevin van Wyk who supported this project from the outset. They lightened the editors' task by searching for poems in their father's papers and digital records. The editors are also grateful to Ingrid de Kok for her advice, and to Kelwyn Sole for helping to locate some of the poems and other useful assistance. The New Coin poetry reading group gave us invaluable feedback on the work in progress. Finally, I thank the School of Literature, Language and Media at the University of the Witwatersrand for supporting my work on this publication.

Ivan Vladislavić
February 2020

from *It Is Time to Go Home*
(Ad Donker/Publisher, 1979)

Metamorphosis

Hardly out of a napkin
into the sixties
Sharpeville
scattered around my father
in newsprint
and me
fidgeting around his work-worn body
asking questions at his shaking head.

That memory has never yellowed
with age.

Now, after June 16
puberty attacks suddenly.
I wriggle bewildered in fertile hair.
I nod my head.
Now I understand.

Anthem for a New Day

I've been woken mornings
by bugs inherent in gauche walls where I live
and squeezed my soporific blood from their gourds
and stayed awake
to tell it to the wick of a yawning candle.

I have shuffled uneasily
between my pockets
and the tattered brim of a tramp's hat
and rushed home to protest on a page.

And the kwela-kwela
that stops before me
in Jo'burg streets – the exhibitionist
and spills or loads to the grille
suppurating bodies that have no pass or say
this and so much more
has made me run home and sob
in the copious apron of exercise books.

This and so much more;
This and Riverlea where I live.
This and Soweto where I live.
This and the Bantustans where I live.
This and Don where I live.
This and Duma where I live.
This and Fhazel where I live.

I live, God, how I live.
How I see suffering
grow more blatant
and shed its wardrobe of disguises – its charity
in the oppressive loneliness where I live
where I live days and lives.

And I record these lives and days
and my friends they have canvases
and torn pastiches
and gloomy nuances
and some shout their hurt from boards
in songs.

We are a black bust moulded from dongas
and dirt and tears
and the ugly smut of oppression.
But we are proud
of our paint and our pens and our gestures.

But oh how I wait for the rapprochement
between gods and men
for a time when souls are ripe
when fresh flags are hoisted high
to write an anthem.

I'd any day abandon this terrible disposition
to do that – my magnum opus –
and you'd be glad, I know
if I'd ask you to write the symphony.

About Graffiti

Graffiti is the writing on the wall
the writing on the wall as at Western
Heroes die young

In Noordgesig you'll see graffiti
Why Lord can't we live together?

Smeared on a wall in Eldorado Park
Love is?

In an alley somewhere
Sex is unlimited

Graffiti is painted on a wall
in District Six
Welcome to Fairyland

Graffiti can move too
Graffiti worms out of noses
of slum kids

Graffiti scrawls in piss
calls itself VD
clogs in priapic places, hurts

Bob Marley shouts reggae
from township cafés
'A hungry stomach
is a hungry man'
graffiti

Graffiti is a dirty child
who scratches for sweets
and himself
in rubbish dumps

Graffiti is the gang
the gang who burnt a nice-time cherrie
and left her behind the shops
for dogs to eat off her left leg

Graffiti is children playing
around broken live wires from lampposts
and the Electricity Department fixing it
after somebody has burnt to death
has been shocked through the conduits
of his slum ignorance

When one black child tells another
'Ek sal jou klap
dan cross ek die border'
it's graffiti

and

When another child says
'I don't like Vorstra and Kruga
because they want us
to speak Afrikaans'

Graffiti screams from a sonorous woman
as the hymens of her sanity rupture

suddenly
in a night

Graffiti shouts from the lips of a township
Kyk voor jou die Welfare sal agter jou kyk

Graffiti calls Soweto Sovieto

Graffiti is a scar on a face

The mine dump is graffiti

A cockroach is graffiti

Candle grease is graffiti

A rabid dog is graffiti

Adrenalin and blood in the township,
that's graffiti

Soon graffiti will break loose
into an ugly plethora
drift into Jo'burg
soil share certificates
deface billboards
dishonour cheques
drown managers, clerks, executives

Soon graffiti will wade into Jo'burg
unhampered by the tourniquet of influx control

Dismissal

All day I missed him.
All day I mourned.
And I spilt ash all around me.
And I spilt time
while I moped in the quarantine
of injustice.

The others went on working.
The others went on singing.
Not a tool was dropped.
Not an eye lifted towards the
dying footsteps...

They had worn black
a long time now.
And always something looking like
gratitude and toil seeped through
but smelt like sweat.
And I moped in the initiation of acceptance.
I'm green to this game.

Winter without You
for Kathy

Here the ruminant frost has eaten the grass
and chatter of pruning's heard.
A painful process pruning, if one considers that
trees are alive and actually grow.
'But it does them good.'
Our local surgeon deploys green fingers
into the shape of a peach to come –
his trade-mark.

Thoughts grope like limbs
search in all directions,
look for the loam of your nearness
your fecund love.

I hold my head high during conversation
so that friends won't sense.
But somehow it droops
to far below
this sinking centigrade.
Winter's long and cold.

I'll last through the pruning.
Wait for the peaches, the pears,
the fleshy fruits whisked away
from the centre of my Eden.

The Dream, the Urge

All of my life till now I've spent
pilfering the purses of crabs
only to discover
a counterfeit dream.

My tooth it has long hankered
after caviare
or fish eggs
harpooned from mouthwatering lagoons
with my own outstretched arms.

And that dream
that dream to creep inside an oyster
and eat
eat until only the rush
of a million fathoms of sea could be heard
has drowned into a stereophonic echo
far too loud for me to bear.

But I have since turned away
from these neap tides.
Now I have an urge, an agrarian urge
for a tumultuous upheaval of earth and blood
into a rich compound of loam.

Then give me the petals
and give me the earth.

A Song of Hope

Black brother
Your lips are parched
and your mouth gapes an anger
wider than a scavenged minehole

Black sister
Your skin bleeds a pus
from a long weary battle
for existence and we lick
your wounds with tears
as long as tongues

Black mother
Your nipples of nutrition
have clogged and droop
down towards kwashiorkor

Black people
Our hearts beat to a lonely
acappella
But one day it will throb
to the rhythm of a drum
And all of Africa will dance

It Is Sleepy in the 'Coloured' Townships

It is sleepy in the 'coloured' townships.
The dust clogs in the rheum of every eye
The August winds blow into all the days
Children play in a gust of streets
or huddle in tired dens like a multi-humped camel.

It is sleepy in the 'coloured' townships.
Wet washing semaphores, then doesn't
and the dirt is spiteful to the whiteness
A Volkswagen engine lies embalmed in grease and grime
(the mechanic has washed his hands and left)
but the car waits patient as rust.

It is sleepy in the 'coloured' townships.
Heads bob around the stove of the sun
The sleepiness is a crust harder than
a tortoise's shell.

It is sleepy in the 'coloured' townships.
A drunk sleeps lulled by meths
Children scratch sores – sleep
bitten by the tsetse flies of Soweto
of June 16
(Noordgesig lies on the fringes of Soweto).

It is sleepy in the 'coloured' townships.
A pensioner in Coronation
lies dead for a week
before the stench of her corpse

attracts attention through keyholes
and windows.

It is sleepy in the 'coloured' townships.
A neighbour's son watches as silkworms
encrusted on mulberry leaves
wrap themselves into cocoons of silk.

It is sleepy in the 'coloured' townships.
It is sleepy in Riverlea and Noordgesig
Eldorado Park, Bosmont, Newclare
It is sleepy in all the 'coloured' townships.

Agrarian Reform

I saw a black man
shake a beseeching voice-box
at whites
crying for coins

And have you heard
of a place called 'Zombie'
where people scream
like poltergeists
crying 'bread!'
and 'water!'
oh I have

But I have also seen
bullets soak into the heart
of a Soweto boy. Saw him
cleave fractured African soil
resuscitate it making loam
of long-eroded Azanian earth

And I know now
the rigor mortis
has not set in
There is still time

'n Ander Ou by die Skool

'n Ander ou by die skool
hy nja net politiek.
Elke speeltyd sal jy hom kry.
Hy politiek net vorentoe.
Van Russians en van Mao.

Hy wietie om te sê lanies is vuil
en darkies is red
en darkies is reg as hulle power maak.

Hy wietie om te sê
Americans is vuil;
hulle vat net ons se zak
maar hulle sal ons never help.

Ander ouens lag.
Ander ouens sê hy's befok.
Ander ouens sê hy's 'n moegoe.

Maar nou die ander dag
toe praat hy according Frelimo.
Al die ouens ziep.
Hulle luister.
Toe sien ek behoorlik die mister wil huil.
Toe praat hy van 'n breakthrough.

Portrait

for Kathy

If I could turn my grey matter
into a palette of pastel shades
change my pen into a brush
and my page into canvas
I'd paint your portrait
create a new old master.

Because you have a smile
that is luminous in a room of dark faces
and a laugh that's boisterous as a binge
and a heart so big
I can splash it all over the canvas
crazy as Van Gogh,
until the easel topples.

Yes, that is what I'd do.
Not write you into a poem
because I'd probably hide half of you
in that part of me that's
speechless
or selfish.

Concrete poetry too
cannot express your beauty
and I can't picture myself
using O's for your eyes
when O's are oh so vacant.

Beware of White Ladies When Spring Is Here

Beware of white ladies
in chemise dresses
and pretty sandals
that show their toes.
Beware of these ladies
when spring is here.
They have strange habits
of infesting our townships
with seeds of:
geraniums pansies poppies carnations.
They plant their seeds in our eroded slums
cultivating charity in our eroded hearts
making our slums look like floral Utopias.
Beware!
Beware of seeds and plants.
They take up your oxygen
and they take up your time
and let you wait for blossoms
and let you pray for rain
and you forget about equality
and blooming liberation
and that you too deserve chemise dresses
and pretty sandals that show your toes.
Beware of white ladies
when spring is here
for they want to make of you
a xerophyte.

Catharsis

Sometimes during long silences
after emotional conversation
about the tenses in our lives
you suddenly lift your head from lifelines
and say:

There were times, Chris
when I wished I was the only child
Then there would've been enough food
to go round.

God how my friend can say things
we all felt at times
but rather left unsaid.

Unemployed

August's hostile wind has buried its hatchet
in doldrums somewhere.
We couldn't care less.
Now a bud makes a mute reveille
calling summer.

We count these unemployed days
like menstruating girls do lunar months.

Dialogue saturates.
Becomes fetid in heat.
I hide my head in the hood of heat.
Split ends.
Incinerate thoughts.

Sometimes you read in my company,
I read in yours.
Encouragement's found in reading
Arthur Nortje backwards
until I reach a ptomained trunk.
'Is this not perhaps where you are now,'
I ask myself and shudder.

We'll pore over ads until jobs find us.
Become ungreased cogs in commerce, industry
or some unimportant auxiliary service
when again I'll write a poem like this.

The Accident

Trains don't swerve
So he lay dead among the sleepers
His body in tiny bits
and people from nowhere came
like vultures
flapping tongues
gaping
    excited
Almost as if they had dropped stuff
    carelessly
They paused
before gathering the pieces
lifting them neatly into paper
    like etiquette
So their hands wouldn't get
    sticky

They carried his pieces away

I hear they had to buy
his body back
to be buried properly
    fifteen rand some odd
A man with a shop paid

It's more now
what with increased rail tariffs

They say it was the first time
he ever belonged

Nightmare

Sharks, I dreamt
had attacked the Island
and were trying to eat away
the men there.

They had chewed gashes
into their bodies
and gaping wounds
where their mouths were.

Now they were trying to
nibble away their hearts
dehydrate the succulence from
their souls
and suck the marrow of perception
from their minds.

I woke up in a sea of sweat
and realized it was true.

Trigger Happiness

Since last year mid-June
whites with guilt-riddled minds
are keeping their guns
out of their holsters
where we can see them
smell the evil
spiralling out of the barrels

They carry them to work
Compare sizes with colleagues
Accountants balance them
in their hands
between ledger and cash-book
entries
Secretaries compare their clicks
to that of their typewriters
Clerks scan their magazines
during lunch-breaks
Pensioners with double-barrelled names
stroke their bores in bed

Whites give whites
guns as presents
Gun shops
have been making a fortune

I've never seen so many guns
before June
They'll never return to their holsters
I know

You Must Never Know I'm Writing You a Love Poem
for Kathy

You must never know
I'm writing you a love poem.
I know you;
you'll almost bribe me with tenderness
so that the poem is a good one.

You'll slide me gently
deep into yourself
and let me nestle
uncaring and content
there in the warmth of your placenta.

You must never know
I'm writing you a love poem.
I want you to find it
only when you type it
with my other stuff.

Now I want you to take it
and roll it up
and bind it
with your typing ribbon.

Your love poem from me.

You who are so good to me.
You who feed me
and keep me warm.

I am happy here;
just being against your navel.

The Pamphlet

Take the pamphlet
Read the bold black words
Know that it comes from a bitter pen
Taste the cheap white paper
Wince as the bitterness attacks your glands

Now drape it over flames
Until it burns beyond all forensic recognition
Yes remember those voices that have to shout
And reason
Out of earshot of the unreasonable

Confession

i would
have brought
you
mulberries
but
they threatened
to explode
their mauve
corpuscles
all over
my
best shirt
so
i ate them

Me and the Rain

Tonight it rains.
After a thunderous fanfare it comes down.
Hitting hard against the rooftops.
Thundering at the windowpanes.
All night through, aggressively
it smashes down upon the earth.
The dogs whimper.
But it rains until it stops.
Pula! Pula! Pula!

Like a catharsis it rains.
Emptying the bellies of the sky.
The September night flows with fright.
I can barely hear myself talk.
I listen instead.
The rain gushes into yards, streets, dongas,
like menses,
spilling forth the stalled emotions of the dry season.
I listen to the rain.
Pula! Pula! Pula!

It rains throughout the night
and people sleep.
But I don't. I hear a rooftop
unclasp itself from a flat and
swing down onto the ground.
And the radio says it's an act of God.
And the insurance company says it's
a natural catastrophe.

And the council say it's not their fault.
And the tenants say it's a sin.
Still it rains.
Pula! Pula! Pula!

I sit in a dry corner at home.
I scratch dandruff and sip coffee.
I think of Duma and Don.
Of Dukuza and Caplan and Fhazel.
I think of Themba and of tomorrow
and I listen to the rain
and my heartbeat;
Boom! Boom! Boom!

The rain is powerful;
it opens graves,
it rains on the Island,
it crawls under cell walls,
it remembers bodies forgotten in holes,
brings them floating into courtrooms:
the habeas corpus.

The rain can coax a flower
out of loam, out of rock.
The rain can uproot euphoria.
The rain can gut consciences.
The rain inspires me.
Pula! Pula! Pula!

Candle
for Caplan

Read brother read.
   The wax is melting fast
   The shadows become obdurate
   and mock pantomimes of you
   laughing through crude cement
   in silent stage whispers.

Read brother read,
   though the wax lies heaped
   in the saucer
   and the silhouettes of gloom
   grow longer.

Read brother read.
   Only the wick shines red now.
   But it is not yet dark.
   Remember brother,
   it is not yet dark.

In Detention

He fell from the ninth floor
He hanged himself
He slipped on a piece of soap while washing
He hanged himself
He slipped on a piece of soap while washing
He fell from the ninth floor
He hanged himself while washing
He slipped from the ninth floor
He hung from the ninth floor
He slipped on the ninth floor while washing
He fell from a piece of soap while slipping
He hung from the ninth floor
He washed from the ninth floor while slipping
He hung from a piece of soap while washing

Coming Home

Rising
from a bed
of aberration
and coir
I greet
the
blinding white dawn
with pride
far deeper
than
the pores
of
my skin
saying
I
am a Black man

On Learning Sotho

for Isaac Sephoka

I was a young Sotho boy then
a baby wetting a layette of words
and all of you laughed boisterously
when I swore at myself
not knowing the difference then
between 'nna' and 'wena'.
And I'd impress all the ladies
with 'dumela ausi!'
or 'moratiwa!' when I was randy.

The words crawled at first
no matter how they tried to walk
among the grown, bombastic men.
Oh I was a child again
joyfully sucking on the tits
of a language new to me
though it had always been
dangling invitingly from Agnes who makes the tea
or Mrs Mabuja who sweeps the office.

Thank you for your patience brother
and your English to guide my Sotho.
I'm growing now
and one day I will be as big as you
and Joseph and Walter and Lucky.
Then I will also laugh when you do
or cry
and understand why.

A Riot Policeman

The sun has gone down
with the last doused flame.
Tonight's last bullet
has singed the day's last victim
an hour ago.
It is time to go home.

The hippo crawls
in a desultory air of triumph
through, around, fluttering
shirts and shoes full of death.
Teargas is simmering.
Tears have been dried by heat
or cooled by death.
Buckshot fills the space
between the maimed and the mourners.
It is time to go home.

A black man surrenders
a stolen bottle of brandy
scurries away with his life
in his hands.
The policeman rests the oasis
on his lips
wipes his mouth on a camouflaged
cuff.
It is time to go home.

Tonight he'll shed his uniform.
Put on his pyjamas.
Play with his children.
Make love to his wife.
Tomorrow is pay-day.
But it is time to go home now,
it is time to go home.

from the Uncollected Poems

Here in Riverlea

Here in Riverlea
houses brood in the winter haze
of smoke and dust
clutching the dry breast of yellow sand
that once weaned the Afrikaner.

Here in Riverlea
it is cold
and it is Monday.
Spouses languish in aftermeal
carbon monoxide kitchens,
discuss Friday – wages.

Here Riverlea
is watched from rooms
by Mary and Boetie
who scrawl asterisks
on mist on panes
marking time, marking
the distinction of their boredom.

Here in Riverlea
the luckier ones maybe
are those would-be Marys and Boeties
trapped in durex in a park somewhere,
a gossamer membrane away
from becoming
(coloured) children.

Spring Cleaning

First we dusted our eyes,
aired our lungs by yawning.
Then we began
detonating rugs
chasing moths.

My brother upset an archive of newspapers
and final reminders on top of a wardrobe.
Mum migrated to the children's room;
said the sun lived there.
Another room almost burst with clamour
and too much double bed.

An old five-cent piece crawled
from underneath linoleum.
Couldn't decide who it belonged to
until someone remembered,
offered to take it in.

I dislocated an old school setwork
from my bookshelf – F.A. Venter se *Bedoelde Land*.
Sniffed at it as if it were Poisonous – Giftig.
Hid it out of reach of children.
Thought it good for safety and rationale.

That night we slept peacefully
sniffing mothballs and summer.

Many Men Have Never Cried

A man does not know where his heart is
until he has cried and felt the tears
stream from the weals of the drenched organ
incidentally passing through the eyes.

A man does not die
the day he rubs shoulders with his grave
and even his soul crawls into segments of humus.

A man dies when he is thrown out
(or when he himself throws a man out)
of the window of a ten-storey building
past the mezzanine of concern or despair.

That's when a man dies
and his country dies with him.

We Can't Meet Here, Brother
for Thami Mnyele

We can't meet here, brother.
We can't talk here in this cold stone world
where whites buy time on credit cards.

I can't hear you, brother!
for the noise of the theorists
and the clanging machinery of the liberal press!

I want to smell the warmth of your friendship, Thami,
not the pollution of gunsmoke and white suicides.

We can't meet here, brother.
Let's go to your home
where we can stroll in the underbrush of your paintings
hone assegais on the edges of serrated tongues.

They Would've Banned Your Eyes, Don
for Don Mattera

They would've banned your eyes, Don.
Don, they would've banned your eyes.
They would've turned into hollow husks
those round brown arsenals
that have outstared a myopic regime
and never blinked in its glare.

They would've banned your eyes, Don.
Don't they see how your eyes have never yielded
under the baton charges, the guns and the teargas.
When the only tears you ever shed
fell in the catchment areas of
Soweto
Western
Sharpeville
to rejuvenate battle-weary souls.

They would've banned your eyes, Don.
Don, they would've banned your eyes.
If only they knew how
your eyes have pierced my heart
so much that I want to
draw blood from the bloodshot,
bury the afterbirth.
Give birth to a new Azania.

Eldorado Park

Often it's hard – even for a poet – to know things.
It was this way with me when I first visited
that ugly ghetto.
Why is it that you hate this dirty bitch of a slum?
I asked myself.
What is it about its grey walls that stink
and its streets that run up to your nostrils?

I still can't say for sure.
All I know is that the whites who built it
came and pissed in its streets
and smeared the walls with dirty things
and retched in the flats,
and before they left, farted, in unison.

Four million big arse-breaths of shit
to make sure that we would not forget
they had put their butts here first
every time we breathed,
so that we could always remember
the kakistocracy.

Oppression

Oppression is a boer giant
who clutches in his hairy hands
his heart, hollow, hard
and shaped like a rugby ball

and who runs amok
from one corner of the country
to the other
leaving a drought in his wake

and us blacks darker
in his great mad shadow

My Mother

My mother could never carry me
while they used the warmth of her womb
to forge their hearts into hatred

My mother could never wean me
because they dried her out
until her breasts were arid tufts of drought

My mother could never embrace me
while she kept house for them
held their children

My mother is a boesman meid
a kaffir girl
a coolie aunty
who wears beads of sweat around her neck
and chains around her ankles

But now defrocked of her dignity she
has broken free of the heirlooms of oppression

and dresses in the fatigues of those
grown tired of serving evil gods

Now my mother is dressed to kill

Wouldn't You Like Me to Visit You after It Has Rained

Wouldn't you like me to visit you
after it has rained
and the fragrance of the earth
is the same here
as where you are
and the billboards and factories
are wet
and there is no rainbow yet
but tiny ones squirm
on tarmac at garages
to compensate?

Wouldn't you like me to visit you
after it has rained
or do you think of my raincoat
dripping onto your bathroom floor
like a weak bladder
and my shoes
making mud of your carpet?

Morning in Sandton

The air is crisp with life.
Every winged creature celebrates the joy of flight.
Insects come alive in the web-footed undergrowth
where I stand knee-deep in dew-grass.
Overhead is an amphitheatre:
drumroll of thunder,
drama of an African day.

Then out sail the Mercedes-Benzes and BMWs.
Behind each wheel a Christian Dior or Pierre Cardin
determined to retain his wealth
driving our Africa.

While rubber-sandalled manservants in kitchenwear
who skulk in the attic of the white conscience
follow suit.

Poem for Dikobe

How did he go about measuring his own time?
I knew him well enough to ask
but there never seemed to be a moment
for such trivial things

Now, dragged into the blackhole
behind bars
at the very beginning of breaking rock
when every moment of fighting for freedoms
counts

the prisoner recalls the countdown to capture
the number of days spent dreaming of it
the spent nights

and he alone knows
that from the turning of the key
he must now begin
to beat his own heart

Joy

for Raymond Suttner

The prisoner walks on his crow's feet
into the laughing sunshine
from his dark web-footed cell
with a bird perched on his shoulder.

And with every step he takes
the rhetoric of heavy keys
that grow in clammy bunches
in the hands of warders
recedes until it is a mere sigh;
God putting his feather on a cloud
after having written yet another chapter
of the sad history of a country.

Outside are the prisoner's sister
and his many friends.
He reaches out and touches them all
like a poem ripped out of the Government Gazette
and grows so tall in his sheer joy
that he even nuzzles the flanks of the clouds.

And everything, everything freezes for a second.
And everything's okay.
And maybe the prisoner was never in prison
for a crime he never was charged with.
And maybe a prisoner was after all never killed
in those cells.

The Ballot and the Bullet

The ballot.
This means voting.
There's this big box.
It has a slot.
Ja, like a money box.
You're given options.
Do you want a cruel government
or a kind one?
A lazy one
or one that works?
You have to make an X
on a square sheet of paper
to decide who is to be
the custodian of the people.
But first you have to identify yourself.
This is easy.
All you need is an ID.
This looks like a passbook;
it has your photo and signature.
Only difference is
you can leave it at home
and not get caught.
That's a ballot.
Now the bullet.
Ag now surely you know
what a bullet is.

Jo'burg to Durban 3rd Class

Joseph, Tsepo, old Mr Setlabogo
and Caplan and I
all got accustomed to each other
one shot through their brandy
and halfway through our rum

And we hoped for the future
and cursed the past
as the stations got more blurred
and our tickets more holes

from examiners who bummed
Black & White whisky
from 'whites only' in 1st class
to 3rd class where we were

with Joseph & Tsepo who are miners
and surfaced awhile to visit their people
there far beyond the gold of the cities
and old Mr Setlabogo
also back from being a man
to being a garden boy again

How we drank
while the train charged across the night
waking up the sleepers

And when it was our turn
for the 5 minute tunnel

I saw the concrete go
this way then that way
And I wondered
if I was coming or going

Your Name

Your name
soughs around and comes to rest about
the shoulders of my soul
and has a fragrance so out of breath and hoarse
that if I were but one heartbeat weaker
I would surely die

But I do disintegrate
parts of me become moisture
other parts dust

Your name is a cottage
carpeted entirely with your pubic hair
through which I tread
inside out
and always onto a gangplank
which leads us into long leagues of a drowning sea

Some Elements of Love

for Kathy and Kevin

Watching him cling to your gourdsfull of milk
I stand poised in the infantsmell
waiting for the loveflow.
And just as it was on his first day
it hits me and I reel in the sheerwet
fountainpleasure of it.

And afterwards, when I
lay him nourishedlimp
across my shoulder
to coax the little stormwinds from him
I see your ear cocked as you listen out
for the love that soughs
in the crook of my arm.

It was like that, remember,
when he was a tiny speckdrop
and there was so much wind
and surf to love with
that you were richsuspicious
and I suspiciousrich.

Landlady

I can almost see her through the wall
that doesn't quite separate me from her
and as I lie down I can feel the ill-wind of her words
blowing through the weeds that grow on my spine.

Drunk, her glasses crash to the floor
and shatter the comfort of my sheets.
I'm about to drift into a fitful sleep
when I turn to my wife as if to make love

and say, 'Let's flee from here.
We could get a caravan, camp in
my mother's yard. Then maybe
I could be a man again.'

'Yes, yes. For light and warmth
we'll attach an electric wire
to your mother's house
like a navel cord.'

The Road

I was four and living at my ouma's
when the news came
as it does to all four-year-olds
from the overhanging vines of the adults,
through the eaves of the wise who suddenly
are not so wise.
Cooking stopped.
Panic shattered the eardrum
of the cup of peace.

All was not well
after that out-of-breath boy
had brought the news
in short telegram gasps.

Quickly ouma wrapped me in a blanket
as cold as the flag of a sad country,
took me away to my mother
whose tears by now were warmer, had more salt
than the dead child, brother, grandchild.

Along the rough road
cobbled with the dirges of beer cans,
tremulous with stones
and filled with more people
than children born to the world that day,
my grandmother walked,
and for her the road grew shorter.
For me, staring over her shoulder,
it grew longer and longer.

Helping My Father Make a Cupboard

My father for the moment
thinks in forty-five degrees,
the sun in twenty-eight or so,
and we wipe our brows
in the knowledge of both.
A festival of sawdust
begins to burgeon
under the persistent drill and saw.

Holding a plank fast,
passing on a hammer,
I descend into childhood.
My mother is tugging at my dirty hand.
We wade through sawdust
up to the butcher's cold counter.
He negotiates,
first with Mum
then with his scale.

Planks marked bottom
and planks marked top
are fitted on and nailed together.
Everyone's opinion is heard
under the noise of the flailing hammer.
Except my father's:
his mouth is stuffed into silence with nails –
enough, at least, to crucify a man
or build a long coffin
for one with half a conscience.

I Have My Father's Voice

When I was a pigeon-toed boy
my father used his voice
to send me to bed
to run and buy the newspaper
to scribble my way through matric.

He also used his voice for harsher things:
to bluster when we made a noise
when the kitchen wasn't cleaned after supper
when I was out too late.

Late for work, on many mornings,
one sock in hand, its twin
an angry glint in his eye, he flings
dirty clothes out of the washing box:
vests, jeans, pants and shirts, shouting
anagrams of fee fo fi fum until he is up
to his knees in a stinking heap of laundry.

I have my father's voice
and his fuming temper
and I shout as he does.
When I walk into a room
where my father has just been
I fill the same spaces he did
from the elbows on the table
to the head thrown back
and when we laugh we aim the guffaw
at the same space in the air.

Everything a poet needs
my father has bequeathed me
except the words.

Football

I watch it on TV, in my lounge,
after Johannesburg has settled down
into the darkness of Gauteng.

When nothing much happens on the box
you can hear the insects
buzzing around the commentator's microphone
like an advert for Baygon Green.

We win and next we play Tunisia.
Where is Tunisia?
They're two nil down after half-time.

The President is our main supporter.
When he's watching we fly through Ghana,
Gabon, Zambia and Zimbabwe
like a child in a Model C school
zips through the alphabet.

The whistle blows. The President
comes down in his ancient swagger
and his brand new football shirt.
He holds aloft the trophy and it glints in the sun.
Enough steel to make the door of a shack.

Dora Tamana

Way back in the fifties
this woman from Cape Town
once stood
where there was only sand.
She took corrugated zinc,
nails,
and stuff that the rich
throw away
and
built what she called
a crèche.
There was sand on the outside
and sand on the inside.
On the outside
the wind hissed
and on the inside
it howled.

Never mind.
She charged a penny a child
and mothers
left their children
in her care.

Every day
she bought some sugar
and some salt
and gave these to the children.
The Dora Tamana Nutrition Plan.

But wait.
The next thing she did was
educate these children.
How?
She took her finger
and wrote in the sand
A B C
and 1 2 3 –
Concave little worms for
the children to marvel at.
The Dora Tamana Syllabus.

My question is:
With all that shifting sand
on the Cape Flats
and with all that wind
called the Southeaster
how did Dora Tamana know
that her words and numbers
would still be there
to this day?

Aunty

Being some seventeen years
younger than my mother,
Aunty was my childhood friend,
running around among the boxcarts
that evolved out of broken prams
and clapping hands
at the birthdays that snuffed out
a year of poverty
and lit a candle to another.

Somehow the years
solidified into decades,
calcified as I learnt
to fling words at them
to turn them into
what I wanted them to be
or not to be
with my romantic
little cuticles
and my fat fingers of fiction.

But the other day,
winter settling comfortably
into its cold threadbare evenings,
I visited Aunty.
She was thin.
There were children everywhere,
bursting from her womb
and filling her tiny rooms
with their far-flung diaspora.

Aunty's life has been
a half circle of childhood
and a hemisphere of adulthood:
two identical halves
of one perfect circle
that bubbles like
the solitary pot of pap
on her stove.

Ouma

When I think of my ouma's house, I remember paradise
where the almighty was always broke
but kept puffing up the deflated clouds
and mending the flagging harp strings in the corner
of her room where the sun poured through the curtains
like the warm, weak black tea that she liked to sip
while she listened to our disputes, kissed our bloody knees
felt our tired foreheads for fevers that sometimes
crept into our games and knocked us out for days.

In the mornings, holidaying at my ouma's,
all my cousins and I rose as one from beds and
makeshift beds among the shoes and mice
and drifted to the warm kitchen
where twenty cups stood like a fleet
of cracked steamboats waiting for us to dip
our buttered bread into the sweet black brew.

And my cousins knew all the film stars, all the pop songs
and some verses from the Bible that we learned
from the Salvation Army with their funny hats
and twangy voices and skins so white and frail
that I did believe if we were all fitted with
our wings one day their shoulders would never
take the strain. They met us every Sunday under
a tree in Hamilton Street where they dispensed
endless tracts of verse.

And often all of these, the verses and the
film stars and the pop songs, came together
in one huge festival that brought every braided girl
and snot-nosed boy from Fuel Road
to Riversdale Street into my ouma's yard
so that my heart almost burst
with all the love and merriment.

And once upon a holiday I came
for my umpteenth – but almost last – time to ouma's
and there was my cousin Richard with a new gun
and without blinking, Ouma, the fastest gun alive
snapped the symmetric plastic pistol in two; one for me
and one for Rich, who didn't mind one bit. Then
we tamed the pillows into horses and shot each other
down until we both died laughing.

And once Ouma, the fastest draw alive,
took me to town to draw her pension. And
afterwards, at the second-hand bookshop,
bought me two books that she helped me choose
by flipping randomly through them.

Although much later I learned that the black words
on the white sheets that swept me across the seas
to adventures in faraway lands were to Granny
like coal strewn across a field of snow.

And now Ouma's hair is turning silver as the stars
drop their tears on her head begging her to come
and live among them in their own version of paradise.
Ouma has been resisting for so long now but soon
I know she'll give in as she always has to all of us whose
empty cups she fills with dreams and golden tea.

Memory

Derek is dangling on the kitchen chair
while I'm shuffling about in a flutter of flour.
Mummy is making vetkoek on the primus.
Derek is too small to peer over the table,
that's why Mummy has perched him on the chair.
His dummy twitters so he's a bird.

I'm not that small; I was four in July.
I'm tall enough to see what's going on;
I'm a giraffe and the blotches of shadow
on the ceiling and the walls
from the flames of the primus and candle
are the patches on my back.

Daddy's coming home soon
from the factory where they're turning him into
a cupboard that creaks,
but the vetkoek are sizzling and growing
like bloated gold coins.
We're rich!

This is the first vivid memory of childhood.
Why have I never written it all down before?
Maybe because the pan falls with a clatter
and the oil swims towards the twittering bird.
Mummy flattens her forearm on the table
stopping the seething flood.

As she does so she pleads with the bird to fly
away, quietly, so as not to ruffle his feathers.
But my brother clambers off the chair
as if he has all the time in the world.
Sensing danger, the twittering gives way to a wail
and the giraffe's patches flare on the restive walls.

Mummy gives a savage scream that echoes across the decades
and cauterizes my childhood like a long scar.

Dreams

It is not dreams who come to me,
it is I who come to them,
like a chrysalis
hot and throbbing they wait for me
to breathe life into them.

Why was that man standing
underneath an umbrella?
Pretending there was rain
in this dry month?
Or hiding from the police?

And what did it mean last week
when I went to the funeral of a stranger
and watched from among the mourners
as his coffin cast a shadow over his
bewildered howling dog?

Many of my dreams escape from me forever
but the ones I remember are so many
so varied
that I am sewing them into a patchwork,
a mantilla to wear to a mass funeral
or a bandanna for a dance to celebrate
the miracle of being alive.

My Mother's Laughter

When I think of my mother's laughter
and how it rang through my childhood
I search for a way to bring it to you
and the nearest analogy of those
sounds that slaughtered the sadness
is this:

When I loosened the string
that choked my bag of marbles
and threw them onto the earth
they captured the sun in their prisms
even as they ran free
and transformed their little windows of light
into coins that I squandered on joy
with all my friends.

On Sundays my mother's laughter
swept the sombre crosses
off the shoulders of the churchgoers
flung us into the streets
with our white shirts pockmarked
with the talismans of tomato sauce
and the brooches of beetroot.

My mother's sheer laughter
filled the afternoon cheering football fields
flew through the nets of the goalposts
and the bags of the whistling orange vendors.

Throughout her life my mother laughed
as she still does today
and even though there was much to cry about
as there is even now
so seldom does she weep
that I am forced to put her tears in parentheses.

My mother's laughter grows out of our house
and people come to taste it.
Citrus mirth, deciduous pleasure. Evergreen.

My mother's laughter runs in the family.

Notes

p.16 *Metamorphosis*

Sharpeville – On 21 March 1960 in Sharpeville near Johannesburg police fired on an unarmed crowd protesting against the pass laws, killing 69 people; see also p.54

June 16 – The Soweto student uprising began on 16 June 1976 in protest against the introduction of Afrikaans as a compulsory medium of instruction in schools; see also p.26, p.36 ('Since last year mid-June')

p.17 *Anthem for a New Day*

kwela-kwela – police van (from isiZulu 'climb on')

Don Mattera (1935-) Writer and activist, often cited as an influence; see also p.41

Duma Ndlovu/Duma ka Ndlovu (1954-) Filmmaker and producer; founder-member of Medupe Writers Association in 1975; see also p.41

Fhazel Johennesse (1956-) Writer, friend and co-founder of literary magazine *Wietie*; see also p.41

p.19 *About Graffiti*

Western (Western Native Township), Noordgesig, Eldorado Park are coloured townships in Johannesburg; also mentioned are Coronation (Coronationville), p.26; Bosmont, Newclare, p.27

District Six – A mainly coloured area of Cape Town; after it was proclaimed white in 1966 the inhabitants were forcibly removed to the Cape Flats; see also p.74

'Ek sal jou klap / dan cross ek die border' – I'll hit you, then I'll cross the border

'Vorstra and Kruga' – John Vorster (Prime Minister, 1966-78) and Jimmy Kruger (Minister of Justice, 1974-79)

'Kyk voor jou die Welfare sal agter jou kyk' – Look in front of you, the Welfare will look after you

influx control – laws and regulations governing the movement of Africans from the bantustan homelands into 'white' South Africa

p.28 *Agrarian Reform*

Zombie (also Zombietown) – nickname for Riverlea Extension

p.29 *'n Ander Ou by die Skool*

This guy at school
he only loves politics.
You'll find him every break.
Just politicking on.
About Russians and about Mao.

He likes to tell us white people are dirty
and darkies are red
and darkies are right to demand black power.

He likes to tell us
Americans are dirty;
they just take our money
but they're never going to help us.

Some guys laugh.
Other guys say he's crazy.
Other guys say he's a fool.

But now the other day
he starts giving us the Frelimo line.
All the guys shut up.
They listen.
Then I see this guy actually wants to cry.
Then he starts talking about a breakthrough.

wietie – to chat, communicate, exchange ideas (see Van Wyk, *Shirley, Goodness & Mercy*, 2004, p.281)

p.33 *Unemployed*

Arthur Nortje (1942-70) Poet; died of a drug overdose in Oxford; his volumes *Dead Roots* and *Lonely against the Light* were published posthumously in 1973

p.35 *Nightmare*

'the Island' – Robben Island maximum security prison for political prisoners; see also p.41

p.38 *The Pamphlet*

'Now drape it over flames' – apartheid legislation allowed for the banning of books, pamphlets and other material considered subversive, which made it illegal to possess or distribute them

p.39 *Confession*

Presumably written in response to the much anthologized poem (1934) by William Carlos Williams:

> *This is just to say*
>
> I have eaten
> the plums
> that were in
> the icebox
>
> and which
> you were probably
> saving
> for breakfast
>
> Forgive me
> they were delicious
> so sweet
> and so cold

p.40 *Me and the Rain*

Pula! – rain; let it rain

Caplan Block was a close friend; see also p.63

Themba Miya – *Staffrider* poet; associated with Medupe Writers Association and Soweto Art Association (see Van Wyk, *Shirley, Goodness & Mercy*, 2004, pp.262-3)

Dukuza – probably Dukuza ka Macu, playwright; plays include *A Matter of Convenience* (1974), *Heaven Weeps for Thina-Sonke* (1976), *Night of the Long Wake* (1983)

p.43 *In Detention*

Written in response to the murder of detainees by the security police, specifically the death of SACP activist Ahmed Timol at John Vorster Square on 27 October 1971 (*Shirley, Goodness & Mercy*, 2004, p.257). When detainees died under torture the police usually claimed they had committed suicide by hanging or injured themselves accidentally by falling. Timol was reported to have jumped to his death. In 2017, a judicial review found that he had been tortured and murdered by being thrown from a window. See also p.52

p.45 *On Learning Sotho*

'nna' and 'wena' – me and you

dumela ausi – hello sister

moratiwa – beloved

p.46 *A Riot Policeman*

hippo – armoured police vehicle

p.50 *Here in Riverlea*

'clutching the dry breast of yellow sand' – Riverlea is clustered around a mine dump, which 'tapers sadly skywards like a huge, depleted breast' (Van Wyk, *Shirley, Goodness & Mercy*, 2004, p.307)

p.51 *Spring Cleaning*

F.A. Venter (1916-97) Afrikaans journalist and novelist; known for novels such as *Bedoelde Land* (1968) about Boer families at the time of the Great Trek

p.53 *We Can't Meet Here, Brother*

Thamsanqa 'Thami' Mnyele (1948-85) Artist, activist and friend, went into exile in Botswana and was killed in an SADF raid on Gaborone; his artwork was used on the cover of *It Is Time to Go Home*

p.54 *They Would've Banned Your Eyes, Don*

Mattera was banned and placed under house arrest 1973-82; the banning order barred him from publishing or working as a journalist, appearing or speaking in public, or engaging in political or social action; it specified the maximum number of people who could be with him in the same room at any one time

p.57 *My Mother*

'a boesman meid [bushman girl], / a kaffir girl, / a coolie aunty' – offensive terms for black women following apartheid racial categories: coloured, African, Indian

p.60 *Poem for Dikobe*

Dikobe wa Mogale/Dikobe Martins (1956-) Activist and writer; jailed in 1984 on terrorism charges just as his first poetry collection *baptism of fire* appeared

p.61 *Joy*

Raymond Suttner (1945-) Activist; political prisoner 1975-83; detained 1986-88 under the state of emergency; the pet parakeet he kept in his cell was on his shoulder when he was released

p.63 *Jo'burg to Durban 3ʳᵈ Class*

'surfaced awhile to visit their people' – under the migrant labour system black miners living in urban hostels made annual visits to their families in the homelands

p.72 *Football*

President Nelson Mandela saw sport as a way of breaking down racial barriers and creating social cohesion. At the 1996 Africa Cup of Nations he wore the national soccer team's jersey during the trophy presentation.

Model C school – former whites-only government schools; after apartheid they became non-racial schools, usually with a better quality of education (and higher fees) than township schools

p.73 *Dora Tamana*

Dora Tamana (1901-83) Communist Party of South Africa and ANC Women's League leader concerned with education and healthcare

p.77 *Ouma*

Stanzas 6 and 7 are the subject of Van Wyk's children's book *Ouma Ruby's Secret*

Printed in the United States
By Bookmasters